I didn't know that some birds hang upside down

© Aladdin Books Ltd 1997
© U.S. text 1997
Produced by
Aladdin Books Ltd
28 Percy Street
London W1P 0LD

First published in the United States in 1997 by
Copper Beech Books,
an imprint of
The Millbrook Press
2 Old New Milford Road
Brookfield, Connecticut 06804

Concept, editorial, and design by
David West Children's Books

Designer: Robert Perry

Illustrators: Chris Shields and Jo Moore

Printed in Belgium

Library of Congress Cataloging-in-Publication Data
Llewellyn, Claire.
Some birds hang upside down ; and other amazing facts about birds /
Claire Llewellyn ; illustrated by Chris Shields and Jo Moore.
p. cm. — (I didn't know that—)
Includes index.
Summary: Gives fun facts about birds—how they fly, feed, hunt,
and look after their young.
ISBN 0-7613-0608-0 (lib. bdg.). — ISBN 0-7613-0597-1 (trade hardcover)
1. Birds—Miscellanea—Juvenile literature. [1. Birds.]
I. Shields, Chris. ill. II. Moore, Jo. ill. III. Title.
IV. Series.
QL676.2.L58 1997   97-10033
598—dc21   CIP AC

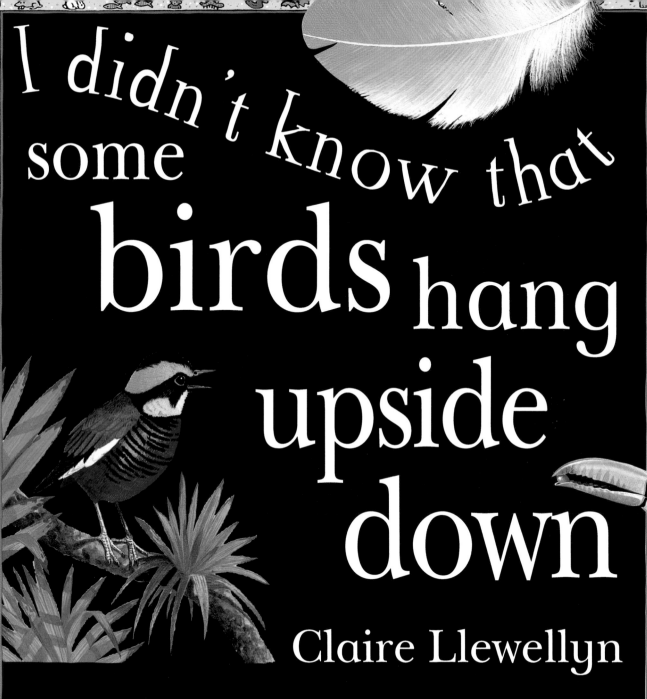

I didn't know that

some birds hang upside down

Claire Llewellyn

COPPER BEECH BOOKS
BROOKFIELD, CONNECTICUT

I didn't know that

Introduction

Did *you* know that some birds travel 600 miles in a single day? ... that some seem to walk on water?... that some can't fly at all?

Discover for yourself amazing facts about all sorts of birds – just how big is the biggest and how small is the smallest, what they eat, how they have babies, and more.

Watch for this symbol that means there is a fun project for you to try.

Is it true or is it false? Watch for this symbol and try to answer the question before reading on for the answer.

The very first bird was a lizardlike creature called *Archaeopteryx*.

I didn't know that

all birds have feathers. Birds are the only animals that have feathers. Feathers keep birds warm and help them to fly. Dull feathers may hide a bird. Colorful ones help to attract a mate.

Peacock

There is an Arabian legend about a magical bird called the phoenix. Every 500 years, the phoenix is said to set itself on fire and is born again from the ashes.

True or false?

Birds are the only animals that can fly.

Answer: **False**

Insects, such as bees and butterflies, fly through the air on fine gauzy wings. Bats can also fly. They are mammals, and their wings are covered with thin sheets of skin.

Fruit bat

Scientists who study birds are called ornithologists. They learn all about birds and the way they behave. But many people are interested in birds and become eager and expert bird-watchers.

The kiwi can't fly. Its feathers are soft and hairy.

An albatross's long, narrow wings measure about 10 feet from tip to tip. These birds don't flap all the time – they glide along on *air currents* rising from the sea below.

Puffin

Albatross

Hold a piece of paper at one end and blow over the top of it. Watch the paper rise. This is how birds can glide. Air passing over the top of the wings gives the bird its "lift."

Storm petrel

Flying is a brilliant way to escape from danger.

Can you find the seal?

I didn't know that

birds have to flap to take off. A bird flies along by lifting its wings, spreading its feathers, and pulling its wings down against the air. Puffins need strong muscles and lots of energy to fly over windy seas.

Storm petrels are tiny birds that seem to walk on water. They dangle their feet in the sea and pick out fish and other tasty tidbits with their beak.

9

I didn't know that

some birds change color. A ptarmigan is brown in summer, but it *molts* and grows new white feathers in the fall. The feathers *camouflage* the bird in the first winter snows and hide it from sharp-eyed hunters.

SEARCH & FIND
Can you find the mountain hare?
FIND & SEARCH

Ptarmigan's winter coat

Birds bathe and *preen* to keep their feathers in tip-top shape.

A bird's feathers weigh about twice as much as its bones.

A bird's wing feathers help it to fly; body feathers *streamline* its shape; *down* feathers keep it warm; tail feathers help it to balance and steer.

Don't try counting a swan's feathers – it has about 25,000! Each feather lasts about a year before it loosens and drops out, and a new one grows.

Barbs are the strands on a feather which hook together to make a flat surface. Zip and unzip a feather by running your fingers up and down the barbs.

11

I didn't know that

penguins can "fly" underwater.
Penguins can't fly through the air
because their wings are too stiff and
stubby. But they make perfect flippers,
and a penguin just flaps them to zoom
through the water.

King penguin

SEARCH & FIND
Can you find five fish?
FIND & SEARCH

Penguins use their wings to slide like a toboggan across the ice.

Birds that can't fly have a problem escaping from danger. Over three hundred years ago sailors landed on an island and found the dodo, a tasty, ground-living bird. Sadly, they hunted it to *extinction*.

Dodo

Emus can't fly, but they run along the ground at about 30 mph. They flash by as fast as a racing bike.

Emu

13

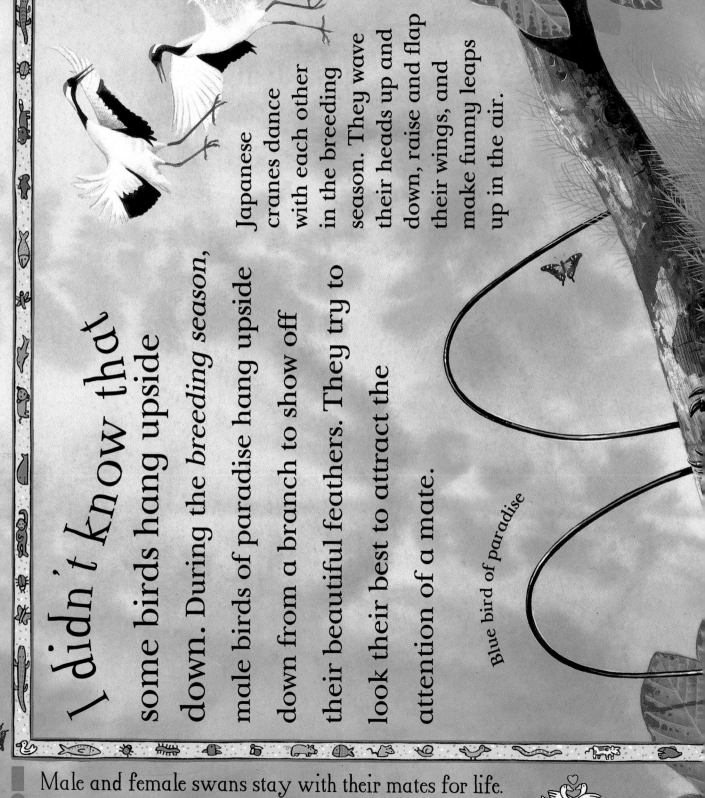

I didn't know that

some birds hang upside down. During the *breeding season,* male birds of paradise hang upside down from a branch to show off their beautiful feathers. They try to look their best to attract the attention of a mate.

Japanese cranes dance with each other in the breeding season. They wave their heads up and down, raise and flap their wings, and make funny leaps up in the air.

Blue bird of paradise

Male and female swans stay with their mates for life.

A male frigate bird shows off by blowing up a big red pouch on its neck.

A male bald eagle dazzles his mate with a fantastic flying display. He swoops through the air, making daredevil dives at up to 100 mph.

SEARCH & FIND

Can you find five butterflies?

SEARCH & FIND

True or false?
Birds sing to attract a mate.

Answer: True
Some of the top singers, such as this banded pitta, like to stay hidden in bushes and trees. Singing out loud is a good way for a male to get himself noticed. And it tells other males to keep off his nest.

15

Rufous ovenbird

An ovenbird's nest is made of clay or mud and looks like an old brick oven. Each bird makes thousands of journeys to collect the mud needed to build a nest that is big enough.

SEARCH & FIND & SEARCH & FIND Can you find 10 weaver birds?

Gila woodpeckers live in hot, dry deserts. They hollow out nesting holes in giant cacti. Cacti are cool inside, and their sharp prickles keep out enemies.

Storks often build their nests on chimneys.

I didn't know that

some birds weave their nests. Weaver birds live on the grasslands of Africa. Male birds use the grasses to weave beautiful hollow nests around the branches of trees. A female then inspects the nests. If she likes one, she may move in!

True or false?
Every bird builds a nest.

Fairy tern

Black-headed weaver

Answer: **False**

Many birds do without nests. The tiny fairy tern lays her one egg on the branch of a tree. Many ocean birds lay their eggs in a hole on the ground or on the ledge of a cliff.

17

I didn't know that

some eggs look like pebbles. Plovers lay their eggs on open ground, in the rocks on a riverbank or beach. The eggs are well hidden because they are speckled and look just like the pebbles around them.

Mandarin duck

Baby birds need warmth, so parent birds keep their eggs warm with their feathers. This is called *incubation*.

Ringed plover

True or false?
Most eggs hatch in ten days.

Answer: **False**
Some birds' eggs hatch in about
ten days, but they're the quickest.
Most eggs take much longer. An
emu's egg takes about
eight weeks to hatch.

Emu chicks

SEARCH & FIND
Can you
find 14 eggs?
FIND & SEARCH

Shell

Baby bird

Yolk

Albumen

Inside the egg, the
baby bird feeds on
the *yolk* and
albumen – the clear
jelly we call the
white. Air reaches the
bird through tiny holes
in the shell.

In many parts of the world, birds' eggs are protected by law.

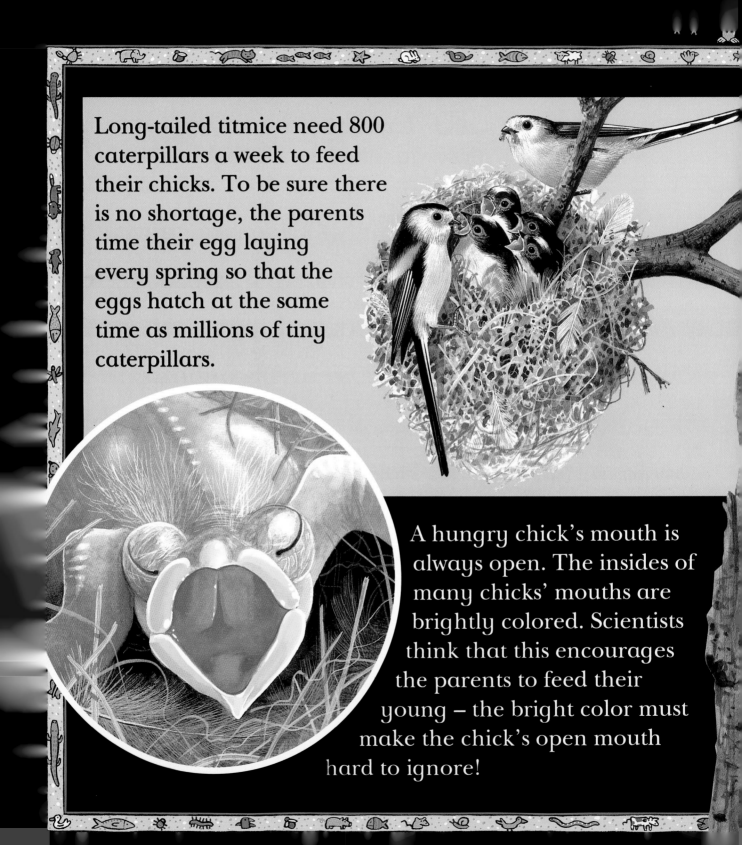

Long-tailed titmice need 800 caterpillars a week to feed their chicks. To be sure there is no shortage, the parents time their egg laying every spring so that the eggs hatch at the same time as millions of tiny caterpillars.

A hungry chick's mouth is always open. The insides of many chicks' mouths are brightly colored. Scientists think that this encourages the parents to feed their young – the bright color must make the chick's open mouth hard to ignore!

I didn't know that

hatching out of an egg is hard work. An eggshell seems brittle and frail, but it is really very strong. A young chick can work hard for many hours, pecking its way out of the egg.

Tawny owl chick

True or false?
All the eggs in a nest hatch at the same time.

Answer: **False**
Owls sit on their eggs as soon as the first one is laid. So the first egg hatches up to one week before the others.

Toco toucan

SEARCH & FIND
Can you find two howler monkeys?
FIND & SEARCH

I didn't know that

toucans eat with tweezers. Toucans feed on fruit. They use their large, hollow bills as daintily as a pair of tweezers to reach ripe fruit at the end of a branch.

The blue jay feeds on nuts, and buries them just like a squirrel.

Hummingbirds suck up *nectar*, using their tongues like straws.

Song thrush

True or false?

A bee-eater never gets stung.

Answer: **True**

Before eating bees, a bee-eater rubs them against the ground to get rid of the poisonous sting.

Bee-eater

A flamingo's beak works like a sieve. The bird sucks in water through its upturned bill. Then, it pushes the water out with its tongue. A fine comb inside the beak traps the tiny bits of food.

A song thrush feeds on small creatures, such as insects and snails. The bird breaks open a snail's shell by hammering it on a stone.

Greater flamingo

Fine comb

23

I didn't know that

some birds kill with a kick. The secretary bird lives on Africa's open grasslands. It stays mainly on the ground and kills animals, such as lizards and snakes, by stamping on them hard with its feet.

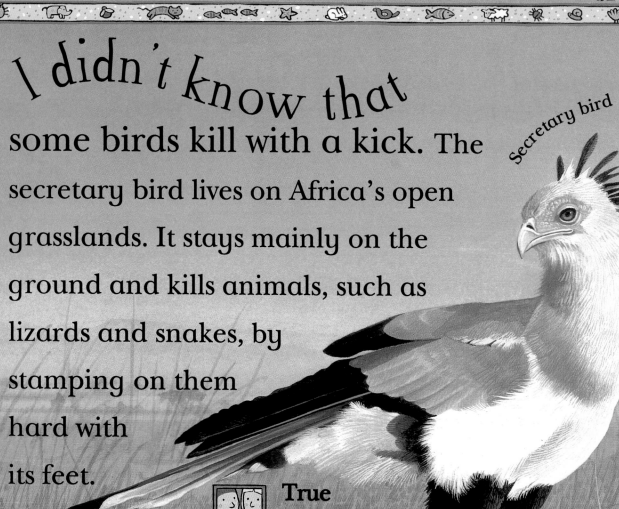

Secretary bird

True or false?

Owls can see in the dark.

Eagle owl

Answer: **False**

An owl's large eyes help it to see well in dim light, but not in total darkness. An owl's sharp hearing helps it to catch its prey at night.

Vultures feed on *carrion*, the meat of dead animals. The birds fly over the grasslands, hoping to spy or smell out a meal. When they find one, they tear it to pieces with their strong hooked beaks.

SEARCH & FIND

Can you find the lizard?

FIND & SEARCH

Vultures

Ospreys are fish hawks. They swoop down over the water, dive in feet-first, and grasp a fish in their *talons*. Then they carry their catch to a nearby tree, and enjoy fresh fish for dinner.

Golden eagles can spot a rabbit one mile away.

I didn't know that

some birds fly 600 miles a day. Geese fly as fast as a car and can go for many hours without stopping. In spring and fall, many of them *migrate* to faraway places, where they can breed or escape bad weather.

Graylag goose

Scientists aren't sure how migrating birds find their way. They may use a built-in "compass" to help them steer, and use the sun or moon as a guide.

Rose-breasted grosbeak

Lighthouse beams confuse birds that migrate at night.

Migrating flocks often fall prey to sportsmen.

True or false?
Some birds fly around the world.

Answer: **True**
The arctic tern flies from the North to the South Pole and back again – every year! That's a round trip of over 22,000 miles (34,000 kilometers).

Arctic tern

Migrating birds often stop off at lakes and *estuaries*. These places are like service stations, where the travelers feed and rest.

Buick swan

True or false?
Some birds fly as fast as an express train.

Answer: **True**

The peregrine falcon is the fastest bird in the world. It attacks other birds in midair by diving down onto them at speeds of nearly 170 mph.

Peregrine falcon

Ostrich

The ostrich is the world's biggest bird. It grows up to nine feet tall. The Cuban bee hummingbird is the smallest bird in the world – it is no bigger than a bee.

Red-billed quelea

The bee hummingbird can even fly backward.

I didn't know that

some flocks contain a million birds. The red-billed quelea lives in Africa in huge flocks of millions of birds. They feed on grass seeds, and can ruin a farm crop in minutes – just like a swarm of locusts.

The bird with the longest beak is the Australian pelican. Its scissorlike bill grows up to 18.5 inches long, and must be very useful when preening!

Glossary

Air current
A rising column of warm air that carries birds upward as they fly.

Barb
The hooklike strands on a feather.

Breeding season
The time of year when male and female birds come together to mate and have a family.

Camouflage
The colors and markings on a bird's feathers, which help it to blend in with its surroundings.

Carrion
The rotting flesh of a dead animal.

Down
Very fine, soft, fluffy feathers.

Estuary
The place where a river flows into the sea.

Extinction
The permanent disappearance of a plant or animal from the Earth.

Incubation
Keeping eggs warm so that the chicks inside them develop and hatch.

Migrate

To travel between one part of the world and another. Some birds migrate each year between their summer breeding ground and their winter feeding ground.

Molt

To shed feathers as they wear out. They are constantly replaced with new ones.

Nectar

The sweet liquid inside flowers, which attracts some birds and other animals and insects.

Preen

A bird is preening when it cleans and smooths its feathers with its beak.

Streamline

To make a smooth body shape, so that a bird can fly through the air more easily.

Talons

The long, curved claws of a bird of prey.

Yolk

The yellow part inside an egg, which provides food for the growing chick.

Index

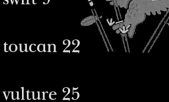